THE PATRIC WALKER
BIRTHDAY BOOK

THE
PATRIC WALKER
BIRTHDAY BOOK

Patric Walker

HarperCollins*Publishers*

HarperCollins books may be purchased for educational,
business, or sales promotional use. For information, please call
or write: Special Markets Department,
HarperCollins Publishers, Inc.,
10 East 53rd Street, New York, NY 10022.
Telephone: (212) 207–7222.

FIRST US. EDITION

Designed and computer page make-up Penny Mills

LIBRARY OF CONGRESS CATALOG CARD NUMBER 92–52564

ISBN 0 – 06 – 016926 – 5

92 93 94 95 96 10 9 8 7 6 5 4 3 2 1

Acknowledgements

The artwork and poems included in this birthday book were the winning entries in a competition held in the *Mail on Sunday*'s *You* Magazine. Readers were invited to interpret astrological signs in the form of either a piece of artwork or poetry. The panel of judges consisted of: *Mail* theatre critic Jack Tinker; author and columnist Keith Waterhouse; actress Sian Phillips; artist Patrick Procktor; *You* Magazine's art director, Jeremy Woodhead, commissioning editor, Peter Watson and sub-editor, Kate Shaw; the publishers, Michael Joseph's, art director, Bob Eames; and me. Again and again I found the image of a sign held by the winning artists and poets went hand in hand, not just with each other, but with my own long-held impressions of that sign. As Jack Tinker said, 'Time after time the winning pieces were the ones that made us smile with recognition. They obviously came from personal experience so they were nearer the truth and were enlivened with wit as well as wisdom.'

The publishers and I would therefore like to thank the winners of the artwork competition: Bob Coelho (Aries); Suzanne Cartledge (Taurus); Jane McLaren (Gemini); Carrie Muskett (Cancer); Karina Moore (Leo); Katherine Johnston (Virgo); Marina Marchione (Libra); Rebecca Tong (Scorpio); Ingebjorg Smith (Sagittarius); Melanie Epps (Capricorn); Jane Askey (Aquarius); and Sarah Steeples (Pisces). The names of the winners of the poetry competition all appear in the text beneath their poems. One artist and one poet were chosen as overall winners of the art and poetry section: Carrie Muskett and Alison Owen.

Patric Walker
Lindos, Greece

Introduction

One day, many thousands of years ago, the Keeper of the Zodiac decided to impart some of his knowledge and wisdom by divulging the 'Secrets of the Stars'.

The whole story, of course, has been lost or misplaced. What we do know, however, is that there are twelve signs of the Zodiac – each representing a particular stage or phase in human development. The word Zodiac simply means – the Zoo of the Heavens.

> The Ram, the Bull, the Heavenly Twins,
> And next the Crab the Lion shines,
> The Virgin and the Scales;
> The Scorpion, Archer, and Sea-goat,
> The Man who holds the water-pot,
> And Fish with glittering tails.

From Aries to Pisces, from Pioneer to Poet, the Art of Astrology gives us a great deal more insight about our own as well as others' characters, natures or dispositions. Above all, however, it enables us to chart our own destinies. We are each blessed with unique gifts and, in the Great Wheel of the Zodiac, have a very special role to play.

There is no such thing as a fortunate or unfortunate birth sign. The exact second an infant comes into this world is exactly when the magic of life on earth begins. What we each do with our lives is called free will.

Say a word of cheer and splendour –
In a moment it is gone
But there are a hundred ripples
Circling on and on and on.'

ANONYMOUS

We cannot ask, we do not choose,
our star signs come with birth,
but if we read them carefully
they guide our life on earth.

Whether water, air, earth or fire
they can help us understand
the reasons why and the secrets of
the future that is planned.

So deal with life objectively,
untap this astral wealth
and use the knowledge it reveals
to find your inner self.

ALISON OWEN

Remembering Martyn
With love

'*Where children are,*
there is the Golden Age.'

Novalis

ARIES

21 March – 20 April

In the northern hemisphere the astrological year begins on or about 21 March at the time of the Spring Equinox – with the sign of Aries.

In his stanzas, Wordsworth, lover of every woodland blossom, did no greater justice to any flower than to the daffodil – the Lent-lily.

> Beside the lake, beneath the trees,
> Fluttering and dancing in the breeze.

Daffodils are the hardiest, showiest and most variable of early spring flowers – and so are those born in late March or during the first three weeks of April.

Ancient astrologers categorised the signs of the Zodiac according to the four elements, and Aries is Fire. It is said to be ruled by Ares – the Greek God of War, which the Romans called Mars. However, it is only because of a basic simplicity and apparent self-confidence that Aries individuals are thought of as warriors. 'The best way out is always through,' advised Robert Frost, born 26 March, 1874. And Andrew Lloyd Webber, born 22 March, 1949, believes, 'You're very lucky in life if you know what you want to do and are able to do it. And it doesn't matter if you succeed all the time or not.'

The Aries character can be likened to one of the earliest song-birds of the year – the missel-thrush. At a time when most other birds remain in snug hiding-places to escape the piercing

wind, he can be seen, perched on top of a tree, braving the blast – which is why he is also called the storm-cock.

As students of human nature – and no one can study the Art of Astrology without laying claim to that title – we encounter what are at first glance either 'strong' or 'weak' characters. The 'strong' are those, like Arians, who do proclaim, lead, challenge and demand attention, who are strong-willed and can turn willpower into action. Above all, however, the Aries individual is honest, pioneering and courageous. In other words, they have a determined and dominant spirit, they know what they want and are determined to get results. And, while it is true to say that the Arian nature may at times appear to be selfish or lacking in softness and flexibility, nevertheless the strength is there to summon up the highest attribute of humanity – the power of the Will.

Many astrologers concern themselves only with the aggressive, independent and domineering personality, but the keyword for the first sign of the Zodiac is 'Aspiration'. What a dull world it would be if men and women were not allowed to see things by the light of their own flames.

To be concerned with one's own being, well-being and welfare is only considered selfish by those who do not have the Aries brand of passion, sense of purpose, individuality and imagination.

Mars may have been the God of War and Pestilence, but he was the child of Zeus and Hera, consort of Aphrodite, and at best the defender of the just and enemy of tyrants.

Of course, every birth sign has its faults, failings and blind spots, and unfortunately the Aries pioneering spirit is accompanied by the innocence of the fool. The March Hare and

April Fool. 'Fools rush in where angels fear to tread' – so the saying goes. This is the mind of the beginner – I am, I exist.

Aries is symbolised by the Ram, and sheep were of great importance in Babylon, the birthplace of astrology. But it is in Ancient Greece that we find Hermes' 'Golden Ram', which could talk and fly and whose golden fleece became the object of the quest of Jason and the Argonauts.

Aries rules the head, and the horns of the Ram represent the unshakeable belief in their own capabilities and self-determination through self-assertion. Direct, courageous, headstrong, impulsive, and both mentally and physically active, Aries is the ignition-key to the Zodiac. But the essence of Aries is an all-consuming desire to be Number One – the best and first past the winning post.

Famous Arians inspire us and, even though maturity of outlook is sometimes difficult to obtain, they set a vivid and perfect example for others to follow by painting on the broadest canvas in life.

April is memory's month. Who, when looking back down the long vista of vanished years, does not remember the springtime of their lives? The springtime and playtime of the years. Dazzling light and sudden shadows. Showers and flowers.

The Aries principle shakes off the winter's restraint and the Aries individual accepts every day as a new adventure. Naturally, a lack of restraint, tact or consideration for others can create so many unnecessary conflicts and so much unhappiness. But when push comes to shove, an Aries partner, lover or friend can always be relied on to share their experience, strength and hope.

21 Traditionally, the First Day of Spring

22

23

24

25 Lady Day
The Feast Day of the Annunciation of the Virgin Mary

26

ARIES

MARCH

27

28

29

30

31

1 *Aperire*, from the Roman, meaning to open; the earth opens to receive seed
All Fools' Day

2

3

4

5

6

ARIES

APRIL

7

8

9

10

11

12

13

14 Cuckoo Day in England, the time when the cuckoo arrives promising summer is coming

15

16

17

18

19

20

Aries

So quick to fly, then fall to earth,
So quick to tears and then to mirth,
You rush away, one aim, to please,
Then comes the fall with wounded knees.
With head so full of daring deeds
You turn away from others' needs.
Then suddenly it's love you give,
All arms, lips and so effusive.
Each morning when you gaily rise
I wait, breath held, for your surprise.
I dare not touch, or swamp with love,
I fear the firm rejecting shove.
One day you'll go, with flight so bold,
I'll lose my Arian four-year-old.

PETER LACEY

Aries

'Live all you can; it's a mistake not to. It doesn't so much matter what you do in particular so long as you have your life. If you haven't had that, what have you had?'

Henry James, born 15 April 1843

'Enter EGO from the wings, pursued by fiends. Exit EGO'

Alec Guinness, born 2 April 1915

'Those who are well assured of their own standing are least apt to trespass on that of others'

Washington Irving, born 3 April 1783

'It is neither wealth nor splendour, but tranquillity and occupation, which gives happiness'

Thomas Jefferson, born 13 April 1743

'Violent antipathies are always suspicious, and betray a secret affinity'

William Hazlitt, born 10 April 1778

Aries

'If a man has no vices, he's in great danger of making vices about his virtues, and there's a spectacle'

Peter Ustinov, born 16 April 1921

'Instruct them how the mind of man becomes a thousand times more beautiful than the earth on which he dwells …'

William Wordsworth, born 7 April 1770

'There is a time for departure even when there's no certain place to go'

Robert Frost, born 26 March 1875

'If you ask me what I came to do in this world, I, an artist, I will answer you "I am here to live out loud" '

Emile Zola, born 2 April 1840

'I'd like to go out with my name above the title'

Bette Davis, born 5 April 1908

21 April – 21 May

The second sign of the Zodiac is Taurus – Taurus the Bull.
And whereas those born under Aries rush in where
angels fear to tread, Taureans meander.

Taurus begins on or about 21 April and ends on approximately 21 May. A time of April showers and May blossoms.
The woods still abound with wild violets and wood anemones
and in many a garden we find forget-me-nots and tulips. The
purple-clad iris vies with the ruddy gold of the wallflowers.
The swallows have returned and far above the lapwing fans the
air. Spring is complete and the promise of summer comes
suddenly. So is it any wonder that Taurus is described as an
Earth sign – the others being Virgo and Capricorn – and is
ruled by Venus or Aphrodite.

The Taurean temperament is touched by the warm
sensuality of the Goddess of Love: affectionate, caring and
capable of making many sacrifices. A perfect example in opera
is Tosca. The Taurean character is committed, determined and
persevering, but also capricious.

Sadly, however, it must be pointed out that there is a
stubborn streak and a tendency to over-indulge in what is
termed the good things of life.

The festival of spring in temperate climates of the northern
hemisphere was celebrated on 1 May – May Day. A time of
maypoles, merry-making and the crowning of the May Queen.
Is it just a coincidence that the creator of Peter Pan was born at
a time of the year when fairies were abroad at night? The

worshippers of the May Goddess frequently wore green, the fairy colour, to encourage the earth to ripen and flower, and green has always been one of Taurus's colours.

There is, however, a practical side to the Taurean character and therefore, though many astrologers agree that Venus, the Goddess of Love, Beauty and Harmony, holds sway while the Sun is in Taurus, one should not overlook the possibility that the Earth is the co-ruler. Down-to-earth, solid, dependable, robust – in other words, the salt of the earth – and the Green Party of the Zodiac.

Do not, however, have the impression that this is a bland or boring sign – Art, Music and a sense of Beauty are very much an integral part of the Taurean make-up. And even when Taureans appear to be at their most difficult, stubborn and intransigent, they can never be described as cold or detached. Whenever one finds the sign of Taurus in a natal chart, there one also discovers a need to learn 'a sense of values'.

'He is well paid that is well satisfied,' declared William Shakespeare, who was born on 23 April 1564. While Sir James Barrie, born 9 May 1860, believed, 'The life of every man is a diary in which he means to write one story, and writes another. And his humblest hour is when he compares the volume as it is with what he vowed to make it.'

Did you know that Frank L. Baum, the creator of *The Wizard of Oz*, was born a Taurean? He was born on 15 May.

Oddly, the Bull counts as a feminine sign, but in this instance 'feminine' simply means tender, intuitive and constant. Once angered, however, Taureans exhibit a sustained fury that is not soon forgotten – a bull in a china shop is a sight to behold!

On balance, though, the Taurean temperament is relatively

placid and peace-loving. Many poets and philosophers born with the Sun in Taurus have enriched our lives with their gentle words of wisdom.

'True happiness is of a retired nature and an enemy of pomp and noise,' wrote Joseph Addison – born 1 May 1672, and goes on to state, 'in the first place, from the enjoyment of oneself, and in the next, from the friendship and conversation of a few select companions.'

But one of my particular favourite writers is Rabindranath Tagore, born 6 May 1861, and to illustrate the true spirit of Taurus, I would select from *Stray Birds,* 'My heart beats in waves the shore of the world and writes upon it her signature in tears with the words "'I love thee"'.

Aries is the 'Pioneer' but Taurus is the 'Builder and the Settler'. It is associated with conservation, natural resources, food, money and possessions, nurturing, growing, building and banking and rules the five senses – sight, hearing, smell, taste and touch. But it is to Taureans we turn for common sense and comfort when times are hard. Taureans plan, programme their thoughts and persevere. And by dint of their own efforts and hard work they invariably achieve a comfortable lifestyle.

The second sign of the Zodiac corresponds to the second house of a solar chart. So it is as well to remember that though Taureans may sometimes appear to be overly or unduly concerned with their creature comforts, they are master and mistress of their own mental household and storecupboards and know full well that the fruits of success have to be won over and over again if they are to be retained.

21

22

23 The Feast Day of St George, patron saint of England. St George became the patron saint of England when he appeared as an apparition in the sky while the Crusaders were fighting their Muslim enemy

24 St Mark's Eve, on which apparitions of those to die in the coming year are said to appear at midnight in churchyards

25

26

27

28

29

30

1   *Maia*, Roman goddess of growth and increase
May Day, originally a Roman festival lasting several days to mark the
commencement of summer

2

3

4

5

6

7

8   The Feast Day of St Michael

9

10

11

12

13

14

15

The Feast Day of St Brendan the Voyager

16

17

18

19

20

21

Taurus

We would like to begin with a chorus
In praise of our dear friend called Taurus
Yes – our 'friend' he will be
Just for so long as he
Doesn't use his sharp hooves to explore us.

ROMER TOPHAM

Taurus

'To dry one's eyes and laugh at a fall,
And baffled, get up and begin again'

Robert Browning, born 7 May 1812

'Where the willingness is great, the difficulties
cannot be great'

Niccolo Machiavelli, born 3 May 1469

'God grows weary of great kingdoms, but never
of little flowers'

Rabindranath Tagore, born 6 May 1861

'That's the wise thrush; he sings each song twice
over
lest you should think he never could recapture
The first fine careless rapture'

Robert Browning, born 7 May 1812

'How poor are they who have not patience.
What wound did ever heal but by degrees'

William Shakespeare, born 23 April 1564

Taurus

'I am not young enough to know everything'

J.M. Barrie, born 9 May 1860

'We're born princes, and the civilising process turns us into frogs'

Eric Berne, born 10 May 1910

'He who sees a need and waits to be asked for help is as unkind as if he had refused it'

Dante Alighieri, born 14 May 1265

'Of all forms of caution, caution in love is perhaps the most fatal to true happiness'

Bertrand Russell, born 18 May 1872

'Youth is something very new: twenty years ago, no one mentioned it'

Coco Chanel, born 19 May 1883

'I've done lots of stupid things, but at least they were my stupid things'

Cher, born 20 May 1945

22 May – 21 June

The third sign of the Zodiac is Gemini – the Twins – communicative, curious, inventive and multi-faceted. The Heavenly Twins shown in astrological illustrations are usually Castor and Pollux, sons of Leda. Sometimes they are depicted as two women, sometimes as a boy and a girl. But no matter how they are presented, Gemini is a puzzlement. Ruled by Mercury, the Messenger of the Gods, on the surface this is the most changeable of signs. Arians say 'I am', Taureans 'I have', but here the key phrase is 'I think'.

Those born in the latter part of May or the first three weeks of June always seem to be thinking, analysing, rationalising or – talking. But one must always remember that this is the time of the 'Flower of Flowers' – the Rose. In the clear light of June, there is no place in all the world more perfect, no home of peace more sweet than that to be found in an old English garden.

However, 'That Spring should vanish with the Rose', laments a Persian poet, and for all their gaiety and apparent preoccupation with the new and untried, Geminians frequently seem to want to linger a while longer in their youth. Author, Poet and Painter has each, in his or her own way, tried to capture the glories of June, when nature dons her brightest robe. When:

> Fair stars that crown a happy day
> Go in and out as if at play.

But Geminians are 'Fair Stars', the Butterflies of the Zodiac because they flit from one experience to another and, for them, variety truly is the Spice of Life. Sometimes restless, contradictory, impatient and critical, but, more often than not, versatile, witty, friendly and eloquent.

Many astrologers tend to believe that to be born with the Sun in Gemini signifies Emotional Detachment, and that it is the head and not the heart that rules. But the emotional nature is kindly; these people could best be described as obliging. They are always ready to offer a helping hand, a little advice, without making any bones about it. They know everybody. Indeed, a wise providence no doubt arranged the Gemini temperament with a view to helping mankind to mix.

'Two persons love in one another the future good which they aid one another to unfold,' believed Margaret Fuller, born 23 May 1810. And Thomas Moore, born 28 May 1779, urges us to remember:

> So Life's year begins and closes;
> Days though shortening still can shine;
> What though youth gave love and roses,
> Age still leaves us friends and wine.

Geminians often have extraordinarily chequered careers. They travel the world, take on every job under the sun, cheerfully undergo the most astonishing ups and downs and count experience as of more value than material gain. Their destinies often depend on the character of the individual they are in closest contact with. At the same time, they have a penchant for having two strings to their bow, be it business or personal interests involved.

However, as we study Gemini we realise this truth. The evolution of man and the planet Earth demands a development through differentiation, and the dualism we see at work in the Gemini individual has a purpose as definite as it is divine.

In mythology, Hermes – or Mercury – was another son of Zeus. His function was as messenger and herald of the gods, in which capacity he is represented as a handsome and agile youth, with winged sandals and a broad-brimmed hat also winged, bearing the caduceus or wand of magic power, a staff wreathed with serpents, which he had from Apollo under not exactly honourable circumstances.

Eventually, Hermes came to be looked on as the God of Herds, also of Commerce. He was, moreover, the guardian of roads, of gymnastic exercises, of clever inventions, such as the alphabet attributed to him; of eloquence, and of games of chance.

An interesting astrological point to be observed is that three times a year, for a period lasting approximately three weeks, Mercury appears to travel backwards in the heavens, and this is when – so astrologers believe – all forms of communication go haywire and we tend to become introspective or circumstances force us to go back over previously learned lessons or experiences.

Gemini is the first of the Air signs, the others being Libra and Aquarius. Therefore, though there is a definite tendency to fly away to Never Never Land, most of the time a typical Geminian is the optimist, the charmer, the story-teller, the party-goer and party-giver, without whose intelligence, enthusiasm and vivacity life would be the poorer.

22

23

24

25

26

27

28

29   Oak Apple Day, commemorating King Charles II finding safety in an oak tree after the Battle of Worcester (1651)

30

31

1   *Junius*, from the Roman meaning family or clan
       The Feast Day of St Erasmus, patron saint of sailors

2

3

4

5

6

7

8

9

10

11

12

13

14

15   The Feast Day of St Vitus

16

17

18

19

20

21

Gemini

It doesn't necessarily follow,
That Geminis are generally hollow
I know one ...

It's not altogether true,
That they don't *mean* 'I love you',
I've heard one ...

It's perhaps something of a lie,
That they never walk, but fly,
I've seen one ...

It's accepted as a ploy,
This imagery of 'joy',
I've experienced one ...
It's just possible to suppose,
I speak as one who knows, as if ...
I am one ...

TERRY BRITTON

Gemini

'When you have eliminated the impossible, whatever remains, however improbable, must be the truth'

        Arthur Conan Doyle, born 22 May 1859

'The true object of life is play. Earth is a task garden, heaven is a playground'

        G.K. Chesterton, born 29 May 1874

'The days that make us happy make us wise'

        John Masefield, born 1 June 1878

'There is not the least use preaching to anyone unless you chance to catch them ill'

        Sydney Smith, born 3 June 1771

'Perhaps the rare and simple pleasure of being seen for what one is compensates for the misery of being it'

        Margaret Drabble, born 5 June 1939

'Too long a sacrifice can make a stone of the heart'

        W.B. Yeats, born 13 June 1865

Gemini

'Many might go to heaven with half the labour they go to hell, if they would venture their industry the right way'

Ben Jonson, born 11 June 1572

'When you get into a tight place and everything goes against you 'till it seems as though you could not hold on a minute longer, never give up then, for that is just the place and time that the tide will turn'

Harriet Beecher Stowe, born 14 June 1811

'What a difficult thing it is to ask someone's advice on a matter without colouring his judgement by the way in which we present the problem'

Blaise Pascal, born 19 June 1623

'Since when do you have to agree with people to defend them from injustice?'

Lillian Hellman, born 20 June 1905

22 June – 23 July

T he fourth sign of the Zodiac is Cancer – symbolised by the Crab and ruled by the Moon. Aries is Fire and states 'I am'. Taurus is Earth and says 'I have'. Gemini is Air and pronounces 'I think'. But only Cancer, the first of the Water signs, proclaims 'I feel'.

Sensitive, sympathetic, protective, Cancerians perceive emotional depths in others, as well as the heights the soul may reach. This is the sign of the Home, of refuge, peace, tranquillity, safety, and simple but sure FAITH. To be a Cancerian is to be on the inside looking out – watchful, and consistent throughout the ever-changing phases of the Moon. The New Moon is a constant reminder that the earth is not a solitary traveller in space.

The Sign of Cancer marks the beginning of summer. In late June and the first three weeks of July one must be up betimes to know the meaning of Tennyson's beautiful lines in the saddest of his lyrics, *Tears, Idle Tears:*

> Ah, sad and strange as in dark summer dawns
> The earliest pipe of half-awakened birds.

As soon as a faint light appears in the east, the earliest pipe is heard. The mulleins, larkspurs and foxgloves seem to be running a race in their upward growth; but the hollyhocks overtop all of them, their beautiful stems rising so majestically from the thick greenery of their root-leaves.

However, do not get the impression that all Cancerians are

soft, pliable and wishy-washy individuals. Far from it. As lovers or sweethearts, Cancerians are quiet, faithful, touchy and extremely possessive, though not unreasonably jealous. They are not given to lightning marriages, though oddly enough in many cases they seem to fall in love before one can say Jack Robinson. Perhaps the most refreshing thing about them is their utter trust in people – once that trust is given. Obviously, therefore, the Cancer soul can be deeply seared by unfaithfulness or cruelty on the part of the beloved.

The Moon has been worshipped as a goddess since time immemorial and the names of Moon deities take one back into other civilisations, perfumed deserts and Greek harvest festivals. The Moon has also been represented as a symbol of fertility, giving us Cybele, Ashtoreth, Isis and Hecate, a mysterious Greek divinity. Although also called Selene and Luna, she is perhaps best known as Diana, or Artemis, Apollo's twin sister, who, like him, drew into her name the character of several foreign deities, one of them that renowned Diana of the Ephesians, whose temple ranked among the Seven Wonders of the World. Artemis let her coldness grow warm for the beautiful youth Endymion, to whom Zeus allowed a choice between death and perpetual youth in dreamy slumber, guarded by the enamoured goddess.

However, Antoine de Saint-Exupéry, author of *The Little Prince*, born on 29 June 1900, believed, 'Love does not consist in gazing at each other but in looking outward in the same direction.' While Jean Jacques Rousseau, born on 28 June 1712, advised, 'To write a good love letter, you ought to begin without knowing what you mean to say, and to finish without knowing what you have written.'

Is there any object in the heavens more beautiful and riveting than the Moon, your ruler?

Modern man is inclined to reject or deride the legends and myths of his early ancestors and, in so doing, disregard so much that is enlightening, spiritually uplifting and worth preserving. But to be born under the sign of Cancer is to have a fascination for times and things past – to trace one's ancestry and to be a collector of mementoes, keepsakes and memorabilia. All the Water signs – Cancer, Scorpio and Pisces – are intuitive, and the Crab, the Scorpion and the Fishes tend to be the first to know what is written in the Stars.

However, there are two traits that are outstanding in Cancer. The first is the quality of receptivity, and the second is that of selectivity. Everything is judged in terms of emotions and feelings. Cancer expresses the paradox of loneliness in the thick of a throng. 'If a man's character is to be abused,' states William Makepeace Thackeray, born 18 July 1811, 'say what you will, there's nobody like a relation to do the business.'

However, fear of ridicule and exclusion sometimes makes Cancerians unduly sensitive to criticism and from an early age they need to be made aware that the world is inhabited by takers and givers. Takers eat better – but givers sleep better.

To sum up, all Cancerians are prophets, philosophers and masters of many moods, both in themselves and in others – the musicians to whose piping all the world must dance. Their true role and function is not only to protect and preserve, but also to revitalise and aspire.

22

23   Midsummer Eve

24   Midsummer Day
     The Feast Day of St John the Baptist

25

26

27

28

29 The Feast Day of St Peter, patron saint of fishermen

30

JULY

Julius Caesar, formerly *Quintilis*, fifth month of Roman (pre-Julian) Calendar

1

2

3 Traditionally, the first of the 'dog days', so called because the dog star rises and sets with the sun during this time

4

5

6

7

8

9

10 The Feast Day of St Antony of the Caves

11

12

13

14 Bastille Day

15 The Feast Day of St Swithin. This Anglo-Saxon saint said he wanted to be buried where he would be exposed to 'the feet of passers-by and the drops falling from above', which led to the meteorological superstition that if it rains on 15 July it will rain for 40 days

16

17

18

19

20

21

22 The Feast Day of St Mary Magdalen

23

Cancer

Lunar leaning, moody tide,
Testing waters for grains of sand.
Loving currents, quick to hide,
Toughened shell for sea or land.

Cautious claws, touching, tasting,
Caring, loving, holding on.
Assurance-seeking, deep-embracing,
Teaching, guiding, put upon.

Centre soft opening up,
With fiery passion in loving cup.

TONY CORCORAN

Cancer

'The highest result of education is tolerance'

Helen Keller, born 27 June 1880

'Love is, above all, the gift of oneself'

Jean Anouilh, born 23 June 1910

'A fool and his money are soon parted. What I want to know is how they got together in the first place'

Cyril Fletcher, born 25 June 1913

'No doubt alcohol, tobacco, and so forth, are things that a saint must avoid, but sainthood is also a thing that human beings must avoid'

George Orwell, born 25 June 1903

'Although the world is full of suffering, it is full also of the overcoming of it'

Helen Keller, born 27 June 1880

Cancer

'Life is full of infinite absurdities, which, strangely enough, do not even need to appear plausible, since they are true'

Luigi Pirandello, born 28 June 1867

'There is no reality except the one contained within us – that is why so many people live an unreal life. They take the images outside them for reality and never allow the world within to assert itself'

Herman Hesse, born 2 July 1877

'Eternity is a terrible thought. I mean, where's it going to end?'

Tom Stoppard, born 3 July 1937

'A thin woman will get wrinkles sooner than a fat one. So the choice is, "Shall I choose face or figure?" My advice has always been – have a lovely face and sit down'

Barbara Cartland, born 9 July 1901

'The cry of equality pulls everyone down'

Iris Murdoch, born 15 July 1919

24 July – 23 August

The fifth sign of the Zodiac is Leo – Leo the Lion – and the Lion says, 'I will'. Ruled by the Sun, the Leo nature or character is said to be regal, dignified, affectionate, loyal and courageous.

Leos are sunflowers. And rich colours have always been associated with the period of the year when the Sun is at home. 'See,' says Leigh Hunt, 'how Heaven loves colour. How great Nature clearly joys in reds and greens.'

And yet, quietly and very gradually, comes the change of season. Does anyone really know exactly when winter begins? The hillside farmers of Greece say it starts on 1 August. Summer's glorious pageant begins to pass in late July and the first three weeks of August, and though a typical Leo may appear to be self-confident – even egotistical – deep down there is an uneasiness and discernible craving for affection and security.

Traditionally, however, this is said to be the Sign of the King, Boss and Big-wig, and is associated with power, gold and heroes – in fact, with most things warm, desirable and to be worshipped. As the giver of heat, light and creative energy, the Sun has always held mankind enthralled. Therefore, is it any wonder that Leo individuals feel blessed, literally bathed in the Sun's rays?

One of the great divinities in Greek mythology, associated with Leo, was the Sun God, Apollo. Adonis, lover of Aphrodite

and for ever associated with beauty, was another. And even today, any outstandingly handsome young man is referred to as an Adonis. Therefore, while one cannot go so far as to say all Leos strut around like peacocks, they are charismatic.

Rupert Brooke, George Bernard Shaw, Percy Bysshe Shelley, Alfred Lord Tennyson, Sir Walter Scott, John Galsworthy, Lawrence of Arabia, Ogden Nash, Robert Graves, Gerard Manley Hopkins, Emily Brontë, Beatrix Potter and Dorothy Parker – the list of Leos who were moved to express their emotions or wax lyrical is endless. 'He started to sing as he tackled the thing That couldn't be done, and he did it,' declares Edgar H. Guest, born 20 August 1881.

And Laurence Binyon, born 10 August 1869, believed, 'A man's language is an unerring index of his nature.'

As the God of Light, Apollo gave men moral laws – his lyre is the symbol of music and song.

The wise sages of Delphi gave the world the two axioms which governed Hellenic life: 'Know thyself' and 'No excess in anything'.

Leo rules the heart, and Leos are in touch with their feelings. Children are equals, and no man is an island; romantic, sometimes rash, but always chivalrous, honest and magnanimous. The Sun is the centre of our solar system, and therefore the light that illuminates comes from the heart.

Popular, friendly, creative, animated and self-confident. 'I make the most of all that comes, and the least of all that goes,' declared Sara Teasdale, born 8 August 1884.

While Dorothy Parker, with her usual mix of humour and sadness, believed:

LEO

Four be the things I am wiser to know:
Idleness, sorrow, a friend, and a foe.
Four be the things I'd be better without:
Love, curiosity, freckles, and doubt.

Leo is the second of the Fire signs and has a lot in common with Aries and Sagittarius, but whereas Aries is a Cardinal sign and Sagittarius Mutable, Leo is Fixed – meaning stubborn or inflexible. But, by and large, Leos not only have the courage of their convictions but the courtesy to allow others to think and do as they please. Added to which, as fond as they may be of pomp and circumstance and, to a large extent, power or authority, there is a sensitivity and love of nature that can best be summed up by this passage from one of the books published at the end of the last century by Madam Sarah Grand:

We do not leave a taste for flowers behind us with our toys. If we like flowers as children, we love them as men. The taste develops like a talent when we cultivate it. To love flowers with true appreciation of their affinities in regard to certain persons is an endowment, a grace of Nature, which bespeaks the most absolute refinement of the mind.

LEO

★

JULY

---

24   The Feast Day of St Christopher, patron saint of travellers

---

25   The Feast Day of St Anne

26

27

28

29

30

31

AUGUST

Julius Caesar, *Augustus*, formerly *Sextilis*, sixth month of Roman (pre-Julian) Calendar

1

2

3

LEO

★ ★ ★
☆ AUGUST

4

5

The Feast Day of the Transfiguration

6

7

8

9

LEO

AUGUST

10

11

12

13

14

15

16

17

18

19

20

21

22

23

Leo

Majestic, resplendent, his face to the sun,
This powerful beast has no cause to run.
He paces with pride, see his beauty unfold,
The king of the jungle, a sight to behold.

His faith is his strength, his glory his might,
Now leading the pack to the edge of the night.
His subjects adoring, they follow behind,
He loves them each one, his loyalty blind.

So look to your king, your leader and friend,
His heart is of gold, love without end.
But beware of the creature whose arrogance shows,
For a king he may be, but a king without clothes.

PAULINE SHERIDAN

Leo

'If I were a girl I'd despair. The supply of good women far exceeds that of the men who deserve them'

Robert Graves, born 24 July 1895

'Children are remarkable for their intelligence and ardour, for their curiosity, their tolerance of shams, the clarity and ruthlessness of their vision'

Aldous Huxley, born 26 July 1894

'The secret of being miserable is to have the leisure to bother about whether you are happy or not'

George Bernard Shaw, born 26 July 1856

'Never look down to test the ground before taking your next step: Only he who keeps his eye fixed on the far horizon will find his right road'

Dag Hammarskjöld, born 29 July 1905

'Children aren't happy with nothing to ignore. And that's what parents are created for'

Ogden Nash, born 19 August 1902

Leo

'Kings are like stars – they rise and set, they have the worship of the world, but no repose'

Percy Bysshe Shelley, born 4 August 1792

'He makes no friend who never made a foe'

Alfred Lord Tennyson, born 6 August 1809

'For memory has painted this perfect day
With colours that never fade,
And we find at the end of a perfect day
The soul of a friend we've made'

Carrie Jacobs Bond, born 11 August 1862

'Childhood is the country that produces the most nostalgic, contentious and opinionated exiles'

Richard Eder, born 16 August 1932

'Most good women are hidden treasures who are only safe because nobody looks for them'

Dorothy Parker, born 22 August 1893

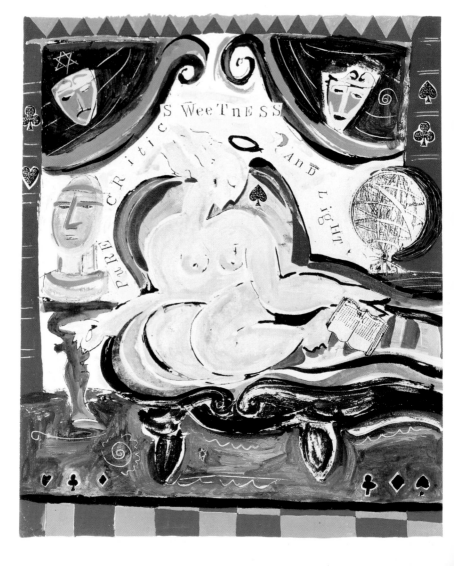

VIRGO

24 August – 23 September

The sixth sign of the Zodiac is Virgo – the Virgin or Corn Maiden. In simple terms, it is related to work and health. However, because, like Gemini, it is said to be ruled by Mercury, the Messenger of the Gods, it is also associated with the world of ideas, communication, discernment and discrimination, and understanding.

> Mind is the master – power moulds and makes, And Man is Mind, and even more he takes the tool of Thought, and, shaping what he wills, Brings forth a thousand joys, a thousand ills: He thinks in secret, and it comes to pass: Environment is but his looking glass.
>
> From *Poverty to Power* by James Allen

When the Virgoan infant enters the world in late August or during the first three weeks of September, the trees are touched with gold and the fitful days are borrowed from summer. For summer is passing away as silently and gently as it came – it is a time of marvellous sunsets and the Golden Moon of Harvest.

This is the second of the Earth signs – the first being Taurus and the last Capricorn. But whereas the Bull happily grazes in the meadow and the Goat finds its meagre meal on a mountain crag, the Corn Maiden co-operates with nature to ensure the cupboard is never bare.

This is the sign of intellect, intelligence, hygiene and harvest-time. Constant questions, refining, analysing, high ideals and

need for perfection seem to have given Virgoans the label 'the Critic'. But the earth's abundance must be put to good use. Work – indeed, hard work – in moderation is in itself a source of happiness. And a typical Virgoan realises how quickly time passes when one is well employed, while it hangs heavily when the mind and hands are idle.

Dr Johnson, Goethe, Tolstoy, H.G. Wells, Mary Shelley, Arthur Koestler and Roald Dahl all prove that Virgoans have a way with words. Hard writing makes easy reading. Plato, surely a Virgoan, is said to have rewritten the first page of the *The Republic* thirteen times; and Carlo Maratti, we are told, made three hundred sketches of the head of Antinoüs before he brought it to his satisfaction. Yet, as J.B. Priestley observed, 'Living in an age of advertisment, we are perpetually dis-illusioned.'

Mercury or Hermes was a prankster as well as the Messenger of the Immortals – the god of Highways, Travellers, Merchants and Thieves – a handsome youth, full of wit and humour and, though not one of the great Olympians, he was honoured throughout Ancient Greece. Apollo taught him how to prophesy and treated him with the affection of an older brother. From Pan he learned to play the pipes, and every portrayal shows Hermes as a young, athletic, graceful man.

However, Demeter, the goddess of the Fruitful Earth, can also be said to be a Virgoan deity, while Hephaestus, the god of Craftsmen, the maker of wonderful, magical things and who tried to keep the peace between his parents, Zeus and Hera, also seems to play a significant role.

In the great wheel of the Zodiac, Virgo sits between Leo and

Libra – the King and the Arbitrator – and represents faithfulness in service to mankind, prudence and unflagging industry. Virgoans come into their own when they allow themselves a few mistakes, when they turn their attention away from miniatures and paint on the broadest possible canvas, when, like another Virgoan – Shirley Conran – they decide that 'Life is too short to stuff a mushroom'.

Georg Wilhelm Friedrich Hegel, born 27 August 1770, declared, 'It is easier to discover a deficiency in individuals, in states, and in Providence, than to see their real import and value.'

But perhaps the lesson to be learned is to be found in the tale of the Old Rug-maker who, when asked why he made a deliberate mistake, replied that the flaw or imperfection was necessary to remind him that he must never be seen trying to outdo the wisdom of Divine nature, which always allows for some mistakes.

24

25

26

27

The Feast Day of St Augustine, Bishop of Hippo

28

29

30

31

SEPTEMBER

Septem (seven), seventh month of Roman (pre-Julian) Calendar

1

2

3

4

5

6

7

The Feast Day of the BLESSED Virgin Mary, observed in the West
since AD 600

8

9

VIRGO

SEPTEMBER

10

11

12

13

14

15

16

17

18

19

20

The Feast Day of St Matthew

21

22

23

Virgo

My true love is a Virgo
And he sometimes makes me mad,
He harks at this, he harks at that,
He's critical and he nags.

I know he loves me dearly
But I wish he'd show it more
When his coldness and aloofness
Have me heading for the door.

But his logic is unbeatable
And his methods work a dream,
He's loyal and hardworking
And more caring than he seems.

N.L. GREGG

Virgo

'It is easier to confess a defect than claim a quality'

Max Beerbohm, born 24 August 1872

'Happy families are all alike: every unhappy family is unhappy in its own way'

Leo Nikolaevich Tolstoy, born 28 August 1828

'The great act of faith is when Man decides that he is not God'

Oliver Wendell Holmes, born 29 August 1809

'An archaeologist is the best husband any woman can have: the older she gets, the more interested he is in her'

Agatha Christie, born 29 August 1890

'The friendships which last are those wherein each friend respects the other's dignity to the point of not really wanting anything from him'

Cyril Connolly, born 10 September 1903

Virgo

'Indeed, now that I come to think of it, I never really feel grown up at all. Perhaps this is because childhood, catching our imagination when it is fresh and tender, never lets go of us'

J.B. Priestley, born 13 September 1894

'However highly you are appraised, always have the courage to say to yourself, I am ignorant'

Ivan Petrovich Pavlov, born 14 September 1849

'There is no disguise which can for long conceal love where it exists or simulate it where it does not'

François, Duc de la Rochefoucauld,
born 15 September 1613

'Adversity has ever been considered as the state in which a man most easily becomes acquainted with himself, being free from flatterers'

Samuel Johnson, born 18 September 1709

24 September – 23 October

The seventh sign of the Zodiac is Libra, ruled by Venus or Aphrodite, and symbolised by the Scales. Consequently, Librans are supposed to be loving, lovable, even-tempered, just and well-balanced.

But in the northern hemisphere this is the time of the autumn equinox, when swallows clear the air in restless and impatient mood, the leaves begin to fall and, as William Bliss Carman said, 'There is something in October sets the gypsy blood astir'.

Ancient astrologers were inspired when they designated Venus, the goddess of Love and Beauty, as the deity to whom Librans owe their allegiance. Lord Byron said, 'Man's love is of man's life a thing apart. 'Tis woman's whole existence', while Madame de Staël believed, 'Love is the history of a woman's life; It is an episode in Man's.'

Be that as it may, much of what has been said and written about the Libran nature or character is utter nonsense. Librans are not well-balanced, uncomplicated, easy-going individuals. How can they be when Venus keeps tilting the scales, tinkering with their affections and telling them that beauty and loveliness are to be prized above all else? Yet recorded history proves that beauty unaccompanied by virtue is like a rose without a perfume!

Aphrodite, though numbered among the élite deities on Mount Olympus and judged 'The Fairest' by Paris was, it must be remembered, responsible for the Trojan War. However, it doesn't do to dwell too long on her misdeeds or misalliances and, to be fair, there is a sweet, kindly, caring side to the Libran nature.

Live and let live is their motto and instinctive principle, but woe betide anyone who takes their affection and generosity for granted, or worse, betrays their trust.

Oscar Wilde, born 16 October 1854, oft quoted: 'Yet each man kills the thing he loves' – tells us much about a Libran in despair, but he also wrote: 'Where there is sorrow there is holy ground.'

'We know well only what we are deprived of', declared François Mauriac, born 11 October 1885. While Thomas Woolf, born 1 October 1885 tells us that: 'The surest cure for vanity is loneliness'.

Finding the perfect soul-mate is of paramount importance for most Librans and many discover in the nick of time only that it is the hardest thing in the grammar of life to learn to put 'mine' and 'thine' in just the right places. Yet that is life's lesson.

Art, artists, painters, designers, colour, beauty, form, grace, charm, music and poetry are very much what Libra is all about. Tosca is a typical heroine and the troubled Orpheus, who glanced back and lost his Eurydice for ever, could well be described as a Libran male, madly in love.

In the great wheel of the Zodiac, Libra sits between Virgo and Scorpio – the pride and the passions – so, is it any wonder that the scales frequently tilt alarmingly? This should also be called the Sign of Open Enemies as well as of Marriage and Partnerships.

There is an Italian proverb that poses the question: 'Have you fifty friends? It is not enough. Have you one enemy? It is too much.' While Longfellow believed: 'If we could read the secret history of our enemy, we should find in each man's life sorrow and suffering enough to disarm all hostility.'

The first six signs of the Zodiac are associated with various stages in our development. The ego, how to earn a living, home and work conditions and so on, but it is only when we reach

Libra that we experience opposites – and the opposite of Libra is Aries. Scratch a Libran and one frequently finds that they have much in common with the purposeful and self-determining Aries individual. Both are termed Cardinal signs. They are innovative and show initiative. Libra is not uncommon in the birth charts of political and military leaders – brilliant campaigners and strategists – and it is certainly true to say that to be born during late September or the first three weeks of October, when autumn tints fall like a glorious mantle on tree and hedge, is to have an uncanny knack of knowing one's own worth: personally, emotionally, professionally and financially.

This is the only sign of the Zodiac symbolised by an inanimate object – a pair of quite ordinary scales.

In *Signs of the Zodiac Analysed* by a remarkable astrologer called Isabelle M. Pagan, and first published in 1911 under the title *From Pioneer to Poet*, Libra is called the sign of the Statesman or Manager. It states that:

> These people hate injustice and unfairness and everything ill-proportioned and ugly in life, and also dislike exaggeration and all feelings that are morbid, depressing, hysterical or strained, turning from them resolutely and refusing to dwell upon them.

How true. But let us now add: no one knows better than a Libran that pride is at the bottom of all great mistakes. That when love and skill work together – expect a masterpiece. That a friend is one who multiplies joys and divides griefs but, above all, that as life wears on the love of husband or wife, of friends and of children, becomes the great solace and delight of age. The one recalls the past, the other gives interest to the future; and in our children we live our lives again.

24

25

26

27

28 The Feast Day of St Wenceslaus, patron saint of Czechoslovakia, the 'good King Wenceslas' of the carol, who attempted to Christianise his nation and was murdered by his brother

29

30

OCTOBER

Octo (eight), eighth month of Roman (pre-Julian) Calendar

1

2

3

4 The Feast Day of St Francis of Assisi

5

6

7

8

9

10

11

12

13

14

The Feast Day of St Teresa of Avilia

15

16

17

18 The Feast Day of St Luke, patron saint of doctors

19

20

21

22

23

Libra

So you think I can't make a decision,
I'm sorry you see me that way.
If you'd just take your foot off my scales it would help,
When they're balanced, the world seems okay.
I'm trying to be diplomatic,
It usually comes easy to me,
But I don't like those colours, please change them,
I need beauty and soft harmony.
I'm not even sure if I like you,
You made fun of my dimples, you see.
So with Venus to guide me, I've made up my mind,
You are definitely not right for me.
    Or are you?

ALISON OWEN

Libra

'In a real dark night of the soul it is always three o'clock in the morning'

F. Scott Fitzgerald, born 24 September 1896

'The critical period in matrimony is at breakfast time'

A.P. Herbert, born 24 September 1890

'There is always one moment in childhood when the door opens and lets in the future'

Graham Greene, born 2 October 1904

'My boy… always try to rub against money, for if you rub up against money long enough, some of it may rub off on you'

Damon Runyon, born 3 October 1880

'The more acute the experience, the less articulate its expression'

Harold Pinter, born 10 October 1930

Libra

'Risk! Risk anything! Do the hardest thing on earth for you. Act for yourself. Face the truth'

> Katherine Mansfield, born 14 October 1888

'What does not destroy me makes me stronger'

> Friedrich Wilhelm Nietzsche,
> born 15 October 1844

'A man can live three days without water, but not one without poetry'

> Oscar Wilde, born 16 October 1854

'A child's spirit is like a child, you can never catch it by running after it; you must stand still, and, for love, it will soon itself come back'

> Arthur Miller, born 17 October 1915

'In politics, if you want anything said, ask a man; if you want anything done, ask a woman'

> Margaret Thatcher, born 13 October 1925

24 October – 22 November

The eighth sign of the Zodiac is Scorpio. Ruled by Pluto and symbolised by the Scorpion, the Eagle or the Phoenix. Here we have all the power, mystery and darkness associated with Pluto, the God of the Underworld. The Ancient Greeks referred to him as Hades, or Plouton, which meant wealth. He was also known as Clymenos, the Illustrious One, or Eubuleus, the Giver of Sound Advice.

But the very first thing to be established is that more saints than sinners are born when the Sun is in Scorpio. Late October and the first three weeks of November conjure up a time when the leaves fall in great profusion, a time of bare boughs and empty fields. However, to eyes observant of nature's wonder, November is a month of great interest; the opal pastel of the misty landscapes is well worth studying. Hour after hour of rain beating down from leaden skies turns fallen leaves into food for sleeping flowers. The earth is a hospital planet and the nature of Scorpio is to take the best of all the previous signs from Aries to Libra and use it to heal, restore and revitalise. 'Our heritage is composed of all the voices that can answer our questions,' wrote André Malraux, born 3 November 1901, while Robert Louis Stevenson, born 13 November 1850, advised, 'If you want a person's faults, go to those who love him. They will not tell you, but they know.'

But, just as many astrologers seem to eulogise about the virtues of, say, Cancerians, the worthiness of Leo, the humanitarian qualities of Aquarius, they simply say, 'Scorpios

are secretive, sensual and to be handled with kid gloves, if not exactly shunned'. And yet, the Kingdom of Scorpio is not only the Kingdom of Power but also power in the most gigantic of tasks – self-mastery. Of course, like everyone else, they have their faults. But, to those who know them well, a Scorpio is a true friend, faithful, loyal, devoted and trustworthy.

Male or female, there is something in the eyes – all-seeing, knowing and understanding. The sad tale of Hades and Persephone is, to many, a typical Scorpio saga of unrequited love, but study it carefully and one comes to realise at some point or other everyone must face what they would prefer to ignore or deny.

So, though Scorpio is the sign of harsh realities, it is also free of make-believe and self-deception. It is a strange mix of the Scientist and the Seer – sorrow and suffering are known only too well and felt acutely, but it is the determination to uncover, discover and discard that amazes and confounds the sternest of critics, rivals or detractors.

From phantasy to pathos – so the change in late October from Libra to Scorpio might be so named. St Martin's Summer or the Greek 'Little Summer of St Dimitrious' is over. And the long winter lies ahead, yet those favoured by Pluto know that though we have in life many troubles, and troubles are of many kinds, some sorrows, alas, are real enough, especially those we bring on ourselves but others, and by no means the least numerous, are mere ghosts of troubles: if we face them boldly, we find that they have no substance or reality but are mere creations of our own morbid imagination. According to Milton:

The mind is its own place, and in itself
Can make a Heaven of Hell, A Hell of Heaven.

Indeed, Milton in his blindness saw more beautiful visions, and Beethoven in his deafness heard more lovely music, than most of us can even hope to enjoy.

We are all apt, when we know not what may happen, to fear the worst but, contrary to popular belief, the Scorpio motto or creed is: 'Foresight is wise, but fore-sorrow is foolish'. It is Pluto, the god of Obsession as well as Possessions, who entreats one to acquiesce without repining, to remember the past with thankfulness and to meet the future hopefully and cheerfully, without fear or suspicion.

There is so much to learn and discover about this frequently maligned sign – Scorpios have a lot in common with Taureans, their opposite in the great wheel of the Zodiac. But whereas Taurus is an Earth sign and Taureans are earthbound, the element associated with Scorpio is water which in turn represents the emotions.

'To love something more than one's self – that is the secret of all that is great; to know how to live for others – that is the aim of all noble souls' – Emile Souvestre

'Subtlety may deceive you, integrity never will' – Oliver Cromwell

24

25

26

27

The Feast Day of SS Simon and Jude

28

29

30

31 All Hallows Eve, the day the souls of the dead were supposed to revisit their homes

NOVEMBER

Novem (nine), ninth month of Roman (pre-Julian) Calendar

All Saints Day

1

All Souls Day

2

SCORPIO

NOVEMBER

3

4

Guy Fawkes Night

5

6

7

8

9	The Feast Day of St Theodore the Recruit
10	
11	The Feast Day of St Menas, who was believed by the Greeks to have the power to find lost objects, particularly sheep
12	
13	
14	

15

16

17 The Feast Day of St Hilda, patron saint of business and professional women

18

19

20

21

22 The Feast Day of St Cecilia, patron saint of music, singers and poets

Scorpio

Some call you scorpion,
Fearing your sting,
The pain and the passion
Engendered

But I've seen you soar
On your terrible wings
An eagle, all evil
Transcended

CLARE O'BRIEN

Scorpio

'A woman without a man cannot meet a man, any man, of any age, without thinking, even if it's for half a second – Perhaps this is the man'

Doris Lessing, born 22 October 1919

'If we're not foolish young, we're foolish old'

Geoffrey Chaucer, born 25 October 1340

'Every child is an artist. The problem is how to remain an artist once he grows up'

Pablo Picasso, born 25 October 1881

'Light breaks where no sun shines;
Where no sea runs, the waters of the heart
Push in their tides'

Dylan Thomas, born 27 October 1914

'I can't quite explain it, but I don't believe one can ever be unhappy for long provided one does just exactly what one wants to and when one wants to'

Evelyn Waugh, born 28 October 1903

Scorpio

'He who praises everybody, praises nobody'

James Boswell, born 29 October 1740

'One can know a man from his laugh, and if you like a man's laugh before you know anything of him, you may confidently say that he is a good man'

Fyodor Mikhailovich Dostoyevsky, born 30 October 1821

'What the hell – you might be right, you might be wrong – but don't just avoid'

Katharine Hepburn, born 9 November 1909

'Scenery is fine – but human nature is finer'

John Keats, born 31 October 1795

'He who thinks himself wise, O heavens! is a great fool'

Voltaire, born 21 November 1694

23 November – 22 December

The ninth sign of the Zodiac is Sagittarius – the Archer, the Sage or Counsellor – ruled by Jupiter or Zeus, the principal Olympian, the Father of Gods and Men, the Greatest and the Best. In the great wheel of the Zodiac, Sagittarius is placed between Scorpio and Capricorn. The first, ruled by Pluto, is associated with the Underworld and 'Divine Power'; the second, under the sway of Saturn or Chronos, is the Great Taskmaster and Old Father Time. But Sagittarius alone stands for 'Divine Wisdom'.

Late November and the first three weeks of December is a time of wild, rough winds. The sparrows keep up a continual chirp and the blackbird and thrush grow more friendly towards us. And we come to realise it is the little that we care to know about the things around us that makes them appear so uninteresting. It is by caring to know as much as we can about the common things around us that make them grow in beauty, and it is by learning a great deal or discovering some of those beauties we know how much there is yet to be learned – how innumerable the beauties still to find.

On a clear night the wondrous spectacle of the Milky Way is visible – the celestial pathway along which the chariot of Phaeton flew. And it was Zeus who metamorphosised the Sisters of Phaeton into poplars and their tears into amber. 'All things that pass are Wisdom's looking-glass,' declared Christina Rossetti, born 5 December 1830, while John Greenleaf Whittier, born 17 December 1807, reminds us, 'For of all sad

words of tongue or pen, The saddest are these: "It might have been."'

But to be born a Sagittarian is to possess a unique ability to face the facts of life fair and square and, in the process, reduce its problems to their simplest terms. 'The Archer' is a centaur, half man, half horse, depicted shooting an arrow into the air, and it is the act of taking accurate aim and hitting the target which tells us a lot about this, the last of the Fire signs. The watchword for the first, Aries, ruled by Mars, is Action. The second, Leo, belongs to the Sun and the keynote is Glory.

But Sagittarius stands for Law and Liberty. Its opposite in the Zodiac is Gemini, whose ruler Mercury was Jupiter's well-loved chosen interpreter and delegate. Yet, whereas Geminians chatter endlessly and constantly change their minds, Sagittarians paint on the broadest canvas in life and believe, 'A man's reach should exceed his grasp, or what's a Heaven for?'

And it is their aspirations which are all-important. 'A great writer is, so to speak, a second government in his country. And for that reason no regime has ever loved great writers, only minor ones.' Alexander Solzhenitsyn, born 11 December 1918.

Travel, they say improves the mind, but this is the sign of the 'Grand Tour' rather than the 'Package Tour'. Both open spaces and places that are seats of learning are the Sagittarian habitat.

Much has been written about the amorous adventures and dalliances of Zeus, but one must remember that he was always found out and taken to task by his wife, Hera. Faith, religion, philosophy and learning are all associated with the ninth house of a solar horoscope and with what is termed the Higher Mind, and no character is so honest in intent as a typical Sagittarian.

SAGITTARIUS

Prophetic, intuitive and capable of sending their thoughts whither they will. By rights, they should be the most self-confident and self-reliant of all the Zodiacal types. And yet no other is so prone to being falsely accused of being inconsiderate and insincere.

However, the Sage of Sages, Socrates, must surely have been a Sagittarian. If not, then Jupiter was strongly placed in his birth chart, for he held that virtue is understanding and that no man knowingly does wrong. More than any other philosopher, Socrates lived his philosophy. Everything that is known about him proclaims the true spirit of Sagittarius: his conversational method of learning and teaching, his lack of affectation, his uncompromising attitude and defiance of public opinion – all Sagittarian traits or characteristics.

Jupiter is the planet of Good Fortune and Optimism, but Benjamin Disraeli, born 21 December, believed: 'Next to knowing when to seize an opportunity, the most important thing in life is to know when to forego an advantage.'

Mark Twain, James Thurber and Sir Winston Churchill are just a few fine examples of individuals who, because they were born at this particular time of year, never lost their ability to laugh, share a joke and make light of what they believed to be ridiculous situations.

'Be good and you will be lonesome'

'There is an old-time toast which is golden for its beauty – "When you ascend the hell of prosperity, may you not meet a friend"'

'Few things are harder to put up with than the annoyance of good example'

23

24

25 Some biblical scholars believe this was the day in 2348 BC when the Flood began

26

27

28

SAGITTARIUS

☆ ★★ ★

NOVEMBER/DECEMBER

29

---

30 The Feast Day of St Andrew, patron saint of Scotland and also of golfers and fishermen

---

DECEMBER

Decem (ten), tenth month of Roman (pre-Julian) Calendar

1

2

3

4

5

6 The Feast Day of St Nicholas, patron saint of youth, popularly known as Santa Claus

7

8

9

10

11

12

13

The Feast Day of St John of the Cross

14

15

SAGITTARIUS

☆ DECEMBER

16

17

18

19

20

21 The Feast Day of St Thomas the Apostle, patron saint of architects

22

Sagittarius

JOVIAN WINGS

Let fly the arrow
On celestial wings
To soar with the eagle
To where nature sings.

Let loose the vision
That guides mortal man
In his quest for the truth
In God's mighty plan.

Let go the fears
That encumber the mind
And open your hearts
To what you might find.

JAMES BROOKES

Sagittarius

'Personally, I'm always ready to learn, although I do not always like being taught'

Winston Churchill, born 30 November 1874

'Fame is a boomerang'

Maria Callas, born 2 December 1923

'Childhood – What was it, really? What was it, this childhood? How else to inquire about it than with this perplexed question – what was it, that burning, that amazement, that endless insufficiency, that sweet, that deep, that radiant feeling of tears welling up? What was it?'

Rainer Maria Rilke, born 4 December 1875

'To live is like to love – all reason is against it, and all healthy instinct for it'

Samuel Butler, born 4 December 1835

'It's our own mediocrity that makes us let go of love, makes us renounce it. True love doesn't know the meaning of renunciation, is not even aware of that problem, never resigns itself; resignation is for beaten people, as beaten paths are for beaten people.'

Eugene Ionesco, born 26 November 1912

Sagittarius

'Oh, how nice it would be, just for today and tomorrow, to be a little boy of five, instead of an ageing playwright of fifty-five, and look forward to all the high jinks with passionate excitement and be given a clockwork train with a full set of rails and a tunnel'

Noël Coward, born 16 December 1899

'The child must teach the man'

John Greenleaf Whittier, born 17 December 1807

'All decent people live beyond their income nowadays, and those who aren't respectable live beyond other people's. A few gifted individuals manage to do both'

Saki (H.H. Munro), born 18 December 1870

'Man has gone long enough, or even too long, without being man enough to face the simple truth that the trouble with man is man'

James Thurber, born 8 December 1894

'Harmony is pure love, for love is complete agreement'

Lope de Vega, born 25 November 1562

23 December – 20 January

The tenth sign of the Zodiac is Capricorn, ruled by Saturn and symbolised by the Goat. The first month of the year derives its name from Janus, the most ancient of Roman gods, represented by a double-faced head to signify his knowledge of both the present and the future. He was the God of the Doorway and protector of all entrances.

The sign of the Goat, which begins on or about 23 December and ends on approximately 20 January, is, like Scorpio, frequently maligned by many modern practitioners of the Art of Astrology.

Now we stand on the threshold of a New Year, and everywhere we look Nature seems to be at rest. Christmas is once again in our midst, and December draws fast to a close. This is the land of winter.

'Through a leafless landscape flows a river.' A time to remember this beautiful line of Longfellow's and the poem in which it occurs, where our friendships are so exquisitely likened to a river – the river of memory – flowing unchanged through our lives like the river flowing through the winter land. And, there is one flower braving the coldest weather – the fragile-looking Winter or Christmas Rose. Many and quaint are the superstitions surrounding it. In early times it was used to purify houses and to hallow dwellings. The ancients also believed that evil spirits were driven away by strewing or perfuming their homes with this plant.

The ruler of Capricorn is Saturn or Chronos. Many celebrated writers, poets and artists have drawn their inspiration from the

CAPRICORN

personalities, characters, myths and doings of the classical gods of Ancient Greece or Rome. For instance, the Owl of Athena or Minerva is associated with knowledge and learning. And the words Jovial, Mercurial, Martial and so on are common parlance. But, unfortunately, poor old Capricorn has been saddled with Saturnine, meaning gloomy and surly. Yet, though typical Capricorns take life seriously, they are not the morose and materialistic individuals astrological textbooks would have us believe. Saturnalia was a time when the woollen bands which bound the feet of the image of Saturn were removed, feasting and jollification began, masters and slaves reversed roles and a good time was had by all. And, what about Father Christmas, Saint Nicholas and Santa Claus!

What is certainly true is that despite the fact Capricorns have decorum, they are also deceptive. Enterprising, shrewd and, at times, materialistic, deep down they have much in common with their opposites in the Zodiac – Cancerians. They are sensitive, vulnerable, self-sacrificing and long-suffering. So, away with the idea that this is simply the sign of Ambition, Possessions, Status Symbols and Worldly Success. Saint Bernadette and Joan of Arc were both born with the Sun in Capricorn.

Chronos means time, hence chronology, and 'Time,' says Carl Sandburg, born 6 January 1878, 'is a great teacher.' While William James, born 11 January 1942, urged, 'Be not afraid of Life. Believe that Life is worth living and your belief will help create the fact.'

Maybe the driving force of this sign is reverence or devotion to the Highest, an earnest desire to attain. Earnest, hard-working, practical, persevering and conventional they certainly are, but there are two points that should be remembered. First, Capricorn

CAPRICORN

is the third and last of the Earth signs, the others being Taurus and Virgo, and, as such, always has a duty to perform, a task to accomplish and a goal in view. In Astrology, Earth represents the physical world, also the senses – touch, taste, smell, sight and hearing – and any true Capricorn will therefore understand these words of Kahil Gibran:

> Then the ploughman said, speak to us of work. And he answered, saying – 'You work that you may keep pace with the earth and the soul of the earth.'

And later on:

> Always you have been told that work is a curse and labour a misfortune.
> But I say that when you work you fulfil a part of earth's furthest dream assigned to you when that dream was born.
> And in keeping yourself with labour you are in truth loving life,
> And to love life through labour is to be intimate with life's inmost secret.

But another salient point that often goes unnoticed is that the Goat has a Fish's tail. Therefore, although this is the sign of Duty, Responsibility and Labour, the tail of the Fish reminds us that the emotions run deep.

Male or female, young or old, love is the light and sunshine of the Capricorn life. 'Love,' as Robert Browning reminds us, 'is best, and our main purpose in life is to preserve it at its best. What is to live, if not to love?'

Finally, 'It may be that we have to lose that knowledge and understanding which children have and then perhaps it comes back to us through living, experience and wisdom.' Louis Bromfield, born 27 December 1896.

23	
24	Christmas Eve
25	Christmas Day
26	The Feast of St Stephen Boxing Day
27	The Feast Day of St John the Evangelist
28	

29

30

31 New Year's Day
Hogmany in Scotland

JANUARY

Janus, Roman god of the portal, facing two ways, past and future

New Year's Day

1

2

3

4

5

6 The Epiphany
   Twelfth Night

7

8

CAPRICORN

★ JANUARY ★★ ★

9

10

11

12

13

14

15 The Feast Day of St Isidore, patron saint of labourers

16

17

18

CAPRICORN
★ ★
☆ JANUARY ★

19

20 St Agnes Eve

Capricorn

The mountain goat looks up, not down
  – It rarely turns around.
It sometimes stays and rests a while
  – Its feet on solid ground.

The climb may seem quite daunting
  – A strain on every limb,
But the mountain goat looks on, not back
  – It has the will to win.

It knows the path is rocky
  – and others may decline,
But one more step, and there it is
  – The top of the world is mine!

R.C. BARLOW

Capricorn

'They, believe me, who wait not gifts from chance, have conquered fate'

Matthew Arnold, born 24 December 1822

'All the world over, the most good-natured find enjoyment in those who miss trains or sit down on frozen pavements'

Rebecca West, born 25 December 1892

'Remember to remember'

Henry Miller, born 26 December 1891

'It is possible that only human beings, of all living species, do not live entirely in the present'

Isaac Asimov, born 2 January 1920

'Natural ability without education has no more often raised a man to glory and virtue than education without natural ability'

Marcus Tullius Cicero, born 3 January 106 BC

Capricorn

'There are people whose watch stops at a certain hour and who remain permanently at that age'

Charles Sainte-Beuve, born 23 December 1804

'How sweet and gracious, even in common speech, is that fine sense which men call Courtesy'

James T. Fields, born 31 December 1817

'The word love has by no means the same sense for both sexes, and this is one cause of the serious misunderstandings that divide them'

Simone de Beauvoir, born 9 January 1908

'Prejudice, which sees what it pleases, cannot see what is plain'

Aubrey de Vere, born 10 January 1814

'We shall have to repent in this generation, not so much for the evil deeds of the wicked people, but for the appalling silence of the good people'

Dr Martin Luther King, born 15 January 1929

21 January – 19 February

The eleventh sign of the Zodiac is Aquarius. Ruled by Uranus and symbolised by the 'Water Bearer'.

Of all the twelve signs, this seems to be the most praiseworthy, idolised and fashionable at the moment, even though whatever is meant by 'The Dawning of the Age of Aquarius' does not appear to be making the world a happier place to live in for Aquarians or anyone else. But the very first thing to remember when considering the nature or characteristics of those born during the latter part of January or the first three weeks of February, is that they are a law unto themselves, unconventional, unpredictable and way ahead of their time.

'The greatest mistake is trying to be more agreeable than you can be,' remarked one Walter Bagehot, born 3 February 1826. But then, Lord Byron, Stendhal, Robbie Burns, Lewis Carroll, Colette, Norman Mailer, Germaine Greer, James Joyce and J.S. Perleman – the list is endless – either believe like Charles Lamb, born 10 February 1775, 'Sentimentally I am disposed to harmony, but organically I am incapable of a tune', or agree with Germaine Greer, 'Every time a man unburdens his heart to a stranger he reaffirms the love that unites humanity'.

Young, middle-aged and old Aquarians have a lot to say for themselves, argue the toss, take risks, espouse causes, resolutely refuse to conform to others' standards but, above all, say what others are unable, afraid or ashamed to convey. Maybe it is because this is the only birth sign that is ruled by the revolutionary planet Uranus. 'However well-organised the foundation of life may be, life must always be full of risks' – Havelock Ellis, born 2 February 1859.

Uranus was discovered or pinpointed by Sir William Herschel on 13 March 1781. This occult and revolutionary heavenly body is a rule-breaker and has often been referred to as the Planet of Destiny. However, if Aquarians are children of Fate, they are also children of Opportunity by being 'All things to all Men'.

It is said to be the sign of Freedom and yet, strangely enough, also of Friendship. Therefore, Aquarians make friends easily, loathe and detest any form of snobbery, class distinction and injustice. And, what's more, they do everything in their power to alleviate suffering. They are social reformers, standard bearers and truth seekers.

'In this world you must be a bit too kind in order to be kind enough,' said Pierre Marivaux, born 4 February 1688.

Aquarians make their entrances at a time when 'Winter lingers and Spring delays her coming'. Birds and animals search for food – and yet, 'Still do children,' says a Victorian writer, 'and common care-laden people seek the faithful and beloved violet family in their sequestered haunts, and draw from them their comfort, inspiration and hope they are so well fitted to impart.' But Aquarians are not shrinking violets – they are Rainbow People and no sign produces so many mystics and missionaries as well as rebels and misfits.

In every respect, Charles Dickens was surely a typical Aquarian. He modelled Mr Micawber on his own father, who went to prison for debt when Charles was only twelve years old. Dickens worked in a blacking factory, and throughout his distinguished career drew on his own experiences.

He could, however, be nauseatingly sentimental, irascible and melodramatic, and at times not much fun to live with. But he cared about the underdog, the poor and under-privileged, and moved the hearts and minds of those who were indifferent to

cruelty and injustice. By contrast, Somerset Maugham, born 25 January 1874, described sentimentality as 'The only sentiment that rubs you up the wrong way' – but the Canadian photographer Karsh said of Maugham, 'He is the kind of Man who has seen everything and doesn't think much of it'.

Yet deep down Aquarians are romantics; why else would St Valentine's Day – the day when birds were believed to begin mating – fall on 14 February? The eleventh house of a solar horoscope represents an individual's hopes and wishes. But it is imperative when dealing with an Aquarian to see the light – their light – without being dazzled by it. For, like bossy Leos, their opposite in the Zodiac, given a chance they take one over. Sometimes the Water Bearer not only douses but also almost drowns newfound friends with affection.

Uranus, the planet of change and rebellion, also marks them out as role-models – movers, shakers and trend-setters – marvellous when they are expected to be monsters and monsters when they are expected to be marvellous. Fascinating, in turn attentive or aloof, vulnerable or independent but never boring.

Aquarius is an Air sign and like Geminians and Librans, Aquarians are born communicators. They enjoy exploring the world of words. Unlike those born under the Twins and the Scales, the Water Bearers bring new concepts to everything they touch. In mythology, Uranus was the God of the Heavens and the Father of Saturn – but it doesn't do to dwell on his odd behaviour. Better by far to end with these words of Stendhal, born 23 January 1783 – 'Almost all our misfortunes in life come from the wrong notions we have about the things that happen to us. To know men thoroughly, to judge events sanely is, therefore, a great step towards happiness,' and, 'A very small degree of hope is sufficient to cause the birth of love.'

21   The Feast Day of St Agnes, patron saint of girls

22

23

24

Burns Night in Scotland

25

26

AQUARIUS

JANUARY

27

28

29

30

31

1 *Februa,* Roman festival of Purification
The Feast Day of St Brigid, or Bride, patron saint of scholars

2

3

4

5

6

7

8

9 The Feast Day of St Apollonia, patron saint of dentists and toothache sufferers

10

11

12

13

14   The Feast Day of St Valentine, patron saint of lovers

15

16

17

18

19

Aquarius

I've forgotten your name, I'm so sorry.
Oh! you stayed with me six months ago?
Ah yes, I remember you're Alfie!
You're not! Well you must be Joe.
Have you eaten? I'll get you some dinner
On second thoughts, hang on a mo,
I forgot to go shopping this morning
And the freezer is now a bit low.
Do you mind if we just have a sandwich?
I've got some nice mild Cheddar cheese
Take your coat off and sit in the armchair
And then do whatever you please.

ANN FAIRMAN

Aquarius

'That great cathedral space which was childhood'

Virginia Woolf, born 25 January 1882

'Security is when everything is settled, when nothing can happen to you; security is the denial of life'

Germaine Greer, born 29 January 1939

'No man, 'Til thirty, should perceive there's a plain woman'

Lord Byron, born 22 January 1788

'A bonny lass I will confess,
Is pleasant to the e'e,
But without some better qualities
She's no lass for me'

Robert Burns, born 25 January 1759

'Getting out of bed in the morning is an act of false confidence'

Jules Feiffer, born 26 January 1929

Aquarius

'The great and almost only comfort about being a woman is that one can always pretend to be more stupid than one is and no one is surprised'

Dame Freya Stark, born 31 January 1893

'When we are planning for posterity, we ought to remember that virtue is not hereditary'

Thomas Paine, born 29 January 1737

'We are always the same age inside'

Gertrude Stein, born 3 February 1874

'At least be sure that you go to the author to get *his* meaning, not to find yours'

John Ruskin, born 8 February 1819

'Fun gives you a forcible hug, and shakes laughter out of you, whether you will or no'

David Garrick, born 19 February 1717

20 February – 20 March

The twelfth and last sign of the Zodiac is Pisces. Ruled by Neptune and symbolised by the Fishes.

'I know you: solitary griefs, desolate passions, aching hours!' To many, these words, written by one Lionel Johnson, who was born on 15 March 1867, seem to sum up the rather sad side of the Piscean nature. The pathos, which is Greek for suffering, associated with being born in late February or during the first three weeks of March, when the snowdrop, called the fair maid of February, peeps up from the ground and the green leaves of the daffodils, or Lent-lilies, also appear.

And, of course, how often is the promise of spring a delusion? For March frequently bears the coldest weather. No matter. Spring is coming and, contrary to popular belief, Pisceans are a hardy lot. They have to be, for nature fashioned them to become aware at a very early age that there would be no joy without pain, the purpose of life is not to be happy, but to matter – to make what philosophical, spiritually-minded folk call a 'Healing Journey'.

And, whereas Aries, the Pioneer, the first sign of the Zodiac, represents Ego, Pisces, the Poet, is the sign of Spirituality. It relates to mysticism – what is concealed, withdrawn and elusive. It really is the sign of the Poet: 'Every possession and happiness is but lent by chance for an uncertain time, and may therefore be demanded back the next hour,' believed Arthur Schopenhauer, born 22 February 1788. And yet, Victor Hugo, born 26 February 1802, tells us, 'Dry happiness is like dry bread. We eat but we do

not dine. I wish for the superfluous, for the useless, for the extravagant, for the too-much, for that which is not good for anything.'

Poseidon, or Neptune, was the God of the Sea. He had equal dignity, but not the power of Zeus. He created the horse in an attempt to be revered by the citizens of Athens but lost out to Athena. His offspring by mortals and immortals included Theseus, and the winged horse, Pegasus.

But, since time immemorial, Pisces has been considered to be the sign of the Dreamer, the Artist, Painter and Prophet.

Sensitive, imaginative, impressionable, tender and compassionate. However, there are two points to remember about 'The Fishes'. First, they swim in opposite directions, signifying a rather complex and contradictory character or disposition – and it is certainly true to say that their strength lies in their ideals and aspirations rather than in their actions – and, second, the Fishes are tied together with a bow, meaning the more they try to be what they are not, go astray or go against their instincts or better judgement, the more miserable they become.

Those who believe in karma explain that Pisces brings a lot of past life's fears and apprehensions as well as knowledge with them. Seemingly careless with money, generous to a fault and ever-ready to devote their time and talent to a worthy cause, yet, strangely enough, some of the world's most successful businessmen and women were born with the Sun in Pisces.

But, it is lines such as Elizabeth Barrett Browning's 'The child's sob in the silence curses deeper than the strong man in his wrath', which make us realise why Pisceans are so precious to those who get close to them and understand what Elizabeth

Taylor, born 27 February 1932, means by this statement, 'Life persists in the vulnerable, the sensitive ... They carry it on. The invulnerable, the too heavily armoured perish.'

From Pioneer to Poet, Astrology is a fascinating guide to the character and characteristics of the human race, and no individuals display more fascinating facets than a typical Piscean. For, Pisces is without doubt the most intuitive, perceptive, creative, versatile and, in a way, the most complete sign of the Zodiac.

'Everybody lives for something better to come. That is why we want to be considerate of every man. Who knows what's in him, why he was born and what he can do' – Maxim Gorky, born 16 March 1868. Also: 'When one loves somebody, everything is clear – where to go, what to do – it all takes care of itself and one doesn't have to ask anybody about anything.'

The opposite sign is Virgo – the Critic – but while Virgoans analyse, rationalise and find the flaw in a masterpiece, Pisces truly strive to make the world come closer to their vision through dedicated service. Their instinct is to trust without question and to give freely.

And what better way to end than by again recalling the words of Victor Hugo, 'The supreme happiness of life is the conviction that we are loved.'

20

21   The Feast Day of St Ursula and her maidens

22

23

24

PISCES ⋆ ⋆ ⋆

⋆ FEBRUARY

25

26

27

28

Leap Year

29

1
Mars, Roman god of battle
The Feast Day of St David, patron saint of Wales

2

3

4

5

6

7

8 The Feast Day of St John of God, patron saint of hospitals and sick children

9

10

11

12

13

14

15 The Ides of March
'Beware the Ides of March'

16

17 The Feast Day of St Patrick, patron saint of Ireland

18

19

20

Epitaph for a Pisces

Meditating
in a bubble bath
the poet hummed
an epitaph
to a self-starred
silver fish
recumbent
on a garnished dish.

As she splashed
the foam did rise
over body, over eyes,

and so she failed
to hear the shout:
'FIRE, FIRE ...
EVERYBODY OUT ...'

ARDA LACEY

Pisces

'I'm not wild about holidays. They always seem a ludicrously expensive way of proving there's no place like home'

Jilly Cooper, born 21 February 1937

'Among those whom I like or admire, I can find no common denominator, but among those who I love, I can; all of them make me laugh'

W.H. Auden, born 21 February 1907

'A boy's will is the wind's will,
And the thoughts of youth are long,
long, thoughts'

Henry Wadsworth Longfellow,
born 27 February 1807

'No man is exempt from saying silly things; the mischief is to say them deliberately'

Michel de Montaigne, born 28 February 1533

'An insufficient talent is the cruellest of all temptations'

George Moore, born 24 February 1852

Pisces

'But if this be not happiness – who knows?
Some day I shall think this a happy day,
And this mood by the name of melancholy,
Shall no more blackened and obscure be'

Edward Thomas, born 3 March 1878

'Why meet we on the bridge of Time to change
one greeting and to part?'

Sir Richard F. Burton, born 19 March 1821

''Tisn't life that matters! 'Tis the courage you
bring to it'

Hugh Walpole, born 13 March 1884

'Make everything as simple as possible, but not
simpler'

Albert Einstein, born 14 March 1879

'Happiness always looks small while you hold it
in your hands, but let it go, and you learn at once
how big and precious it is'

Maxim Gorky, born 16 March 1868